T0208928

Food for Thought

Raising Confident Kids One
Conversation at a Time

Kim Moog

WESTBOW
PRESS®
A DIVISION OF THOMAS NELSON
& ZONDERVAN

WestBow Press books may be ordered through booksellers or by contacting:

WestBow Press
A Division of Thomas Nelson & Zondervan
1663 Liberty Drive
Bloomington, IN 47403
www.westbowpress.com
1 (866) 928-1240

Scripture quotations are taken from The Holy Bible, New International Version®, NIV® Copyright © 1973, 1978, 1984, 2011 by Biblica, Inc.® Used by permission. All rights reserved worldwide.

ISBN: 978-1-9736-9646-9 (sc)
ISBN: 978-1-9736-9647-6 (e)

Library of Congress Control Number: 2020914237

Print information available on the last page.

WestBow Press rev. date: 08/10/2020

For Laura, Sarah and Savannah, I am honored to be your Mom, and I love each of you for the incredible woman you have become.

Contents

Introduction

As a parent, trying to raise successful adults, besides faith, what is the greatest asset you can build inside your children? To me the answer is *a confident voice*.

I remember one particular summer day many years ago when I sat in my bedroom alone feeling defeated after just having had a screaming match with my oldest daughter, Laura, who was eleven or twelve at the time. While I sat on the bed lamenting how poorly I had handled the situation with my daughter, I noticed all of the parenting books that I owned on the shelf directly in front of me. They made me feel even worse. I realized that I had read them all, but none of them had managed to show me any practical ways to apply the concepts they taught to the everyday interactions I had with my children.

I had purchased and read all of those parenting books because I'd believe that, as parents, we are given the privilege and carry the burden of creating the world's greatest commodity—productive adult members of society. I had also taken to heart the realization that the only thing my children will get to take with them to heaven is their *character*.

The dilemma I was facing was that I understood that character training is not something you can cram for. Like typing or playing the piano, your character has to work at a subconscious level; lasting character training has to be absorbed slowly, in small bite-size pieces. I felt like I had never found the time or opportunities to feed my girls these pieces. And I had no idea where or how to begin.

I pulled the parenting books off the shelf and began thumbing through them, in hopes of gleaning something practical I could use. While I skimmed the pages, the memory of a recent conversation I'd had with my husband surfaced. It was an election year, and we had recently been discussing the fact that neither his parents nor mine had the same political beliefs that we held. In fact, we had different opinions about many of life's principles from our parents. How could that be?

Children absorb so much of what is going on around them. Whether it is from their parents, their siblings, the schools and churches they attend, or the sports and activities they participate in, they are having experiences and forming beliefs and opinions through them. As parents, unless we intentionally teach our children the values and beliefs that we want them to have, our children will form their own set of beliefs and values somewhere else. Sometimes people get lucky, and the child turns out to be a successful adult—loved and respected by his peers through very little adult training from his parents. If you ask me, though, that's a pretty risky chance to take when a child's—and your whole family's—health, happiness, and eternity are at stake.

The problem is that kids can smell a lecture from a mile away, and when their defenses go up, their ears can hear you, but their hearts aren't listening. However, by asking them questions instead of lecturing them, children have to create and form their answers; in doing so, they have to take ownership of those answers.

It occurred to me that asking my girls open-ended questions would facilitate the opportunities to teach them the concepts I so desperately wanted them to understand—faith, graciousness, humility, a generous heart, an attitude of gratitude; you get the idea.

I discussed this idea with Michael, and he agreed saying,

"Yeah, I don't want the first conversation we have with our girls about drinking to be on a night they come home drunk."

So I set about writing as many open-ended questions as I could think of that would prompt those kinds of conversations. Then, as we prepared dinner each night, the questions would be set on the table along with the forks, knives, spoons, plates, and salad dressing. We would each take turns reading the question. Then each person at the table was allowed to voice his or her opinion on the subject.

In those dinner table conversations, Michael and I taught our girls some extremely valuable life lessons. Not only were we able to teach them what we believed about certain things, but we taught them that it was okay to have a different opinion as well. We respected their right to feel differently than we did. Sometimes Michael and I each held different opinions and answers to the question, and we were able to teach our girls how we could disagree with each other unemotionally and intelligently, without fighting.

They taught us some things as well. Occasionally, they would even change our minds about an issue, which let them know that they could change other people's opinion by intelligently making a plausible argument. It also taught them that we value their thoughts and opinions. Occasionally, we would have guests sitting at our dinner table, and it was fun and interesting to hear other people's input as well.

I will warn you that this will not make your children into saints. In fact, it might seem like it makes your parenting situation worse because your children will get used to being able to freely voice their opinions. They probably will take some opportunities to freely express some of their negative emotions instead of suppressing them. But that's okay. I believe one of the greatest gifts you can give your children is to have them leave home without carrying a lot of emotional baggage around with them the rest of their lives about things they could have said but never did.

Also—not often, but occasionally—one of our girls would say, "I don't want to do a discussion question tonight." So we would let it go. I never wanted them to feel like we were forcing these conversations down their throats.

One of the other great benefits of these conversations was to hear my girls freely asking their friends and other adults these kinds of open-ended questions and listening sincerely to the person's answers. Sometimes one of the girls would come to the dinner table saying, "I have the discussion question for tonight!"

Eventually, we knew we had been doing the right things when one of our girls would come to us privately and ask us our opinions about a tough moral issue they were struggling to sort out. They would willingly share their viewpoints and listen to ours, without fear of admonishment.

Ultimately, our success has been to see three beautiful young women walk into life as intelligent, confident, and strong, godly adults who know with confidence that God and their parents love them very much!

I could go on naming all of the positive conversations and experiences we shared with our children, and that would be a wonderful trip down memory lane for me. But, instead of having you take my word for it, my hopes and prayers for you, your family, and *especially* your children are that you will make the commitment to start asking some of these open-ended questions—whether at the dinner table, on a road trip, or maybe even at your next family reunion. You don't have to use them all, but take your pick. Choose the ones you would like to try, and give it a shot. You're going to eat dinner anyway; you might as well create some great memories to go along with it. I guarantee the memories of those conversations will last far longer than the memory of that food will; who knows? You might even learn something!

Take care and God's many blessings!
Kim Moog

Note: The red flag icons 🚩 listed with some of the questions are an indicator that the question should probably wait to be asked until the child is old enough to openly discuss it. It is up to you to know when you believe your children are old enough to discuss these. Additionally, we have included an addendum list of some more basic and fun questions to ask in case you have a preschooler there who is feeling left out.

And if your kids give you some answers that you are unsure of how to handle or if they have questions of their own that you need some advice on how to answer, please reach out to www. food4thought.family. We will try to give you an applicable answer or at least get you to someone who can provide you with some optional answers.

If you have preteens or teenage children, *please* help them each find at least one other trusted adult who can pour into them. This should be someone your children can turn to and ask questions <u>when</u>—not if—your children begin to look to other adults for advice besides their parents.

JANUARY 1—What is a New Year's resolution? Why do people make them? Do you think it's a good idea to make one? Why or why not?

JANUARY 2—Do people learn new things the same way? How are learning styles the same or different? Why do you think that is?

JANUARY 3—What is your favorite flavor of ice cream? (Wait for everyone to answer.) Is it okay if the answers are all different or if some are the same? Why do you think so?

JANUARY 4—Everyone here has to tell a joke. Do you think it's important to find humor in life? Why or why not?

JANUARY 5—Do you believe God loves you? How do you know?

JANUARY 6—Can you go looking for or find joy and happiness? If so, how? If not, why not?

JANUARY 7—Do you think it's important to forgive others? Why or why not? What about yourself?

JANUARY 8—What other ways besides reading a book can you learn more about a place, a thing, or an event?

JANUARY 9—What can you do when you are having a really bad day to keep a happy attitude anyway? (Remember: attitudes are contagious!)

JANUARY 10—Is it important that we love and care for each other? Why or why not?

JANUARY 11—Do you think it's easy or hard to hate someone? Why do you think so?

JANUARY 12—Can you name something nice that you have done for someone else today? Do you think that it's important that we do something for another person *every* day? Why or why not?

JANUARY 13—Do you believe that Dad and Mom love you? How do you know?

JANUARY 14—Who has helped you today? Did you say thank you to him or her? Is it important to thank others? Why or why not?

JANUARY 15—If someone is mean to you, does that make it all right for you to be mean to him or her back? Why or why not?

JANUARY 16—Are there things that you would like to pray about? Why or why not? Do you believe that God will answer your prayer?

JANUARY 17—What makes someone a hero? Do you know any?

JANUARY 18—Martin Luther King said, "Nonviolence is a powerful and just weapon. Indeed, it is a weapon unique in history, which cuts without wounding and enables the man who wields it." What do you think he meant by that and do you agree with him? Why or why not?

JANUARY 19—If someone asked, "What do your parents do for a job?" what would you say?

JANUARY 20—Why do you think people have such different opinions? Is it good or bad that we have so many different opinions in the world? Why do you think that?

JANUARY 21—What is the best thing that ever happened to you? What made it so wonderful?

JANUARY 22—Do you think it is important to spend time outside every day? Why or why not?

JANUARY 23—Can you think of a time when you believed something only to find out later that it wasn't true? When you found out the truth, how did you feel? Did you learn anything from that experience? If so, what?

JANUARY 24—Which season of the year is your favorite? Why? Why do you think God gave us four seasons?

JANUARY 25—What do you think Mom was like as a child? What did she like to do? What about Dad?

JANUARY 26—What do you think makes humankind different from other animals? Do you think that is a good thing or a bad thing? Why do you think that?

JANUARY 27—Is it important to stand up for what we believe in? Why or why not?

JANUARY 28—What would you do if one of your friends was being teased or mocked for standing up for what was right? Would you defend him or her and risk being teased too? Why or why not?

JANUARY 29—What is tithing? Do you think it is important to tithe? Why or why not? Does God need money?

JANUARY 30—Who are some people who have done extraordinary things? Why do you think they were able to do something extraordinary?

JANUARY 31—Why do you think one of the Ten Commandments is that we should have a day of rest?

FEBRUARY 1—What are some ways that you can show your siblings or other family members that you love them?

FEBRUARY 2—What if a friend asked you to tell him or her the truth about something and you knew that the truth would really hurt your friend's feelings? Would you still tell the truth? Why or why not?

FEBRUARY 3—Is it important to have and to keep a sense of humor about life? Why or why not?

FEBRUARY 4—What are some things that make you happy? Where do you think happiness comes from?

FEBRUARY 5—Can you name someone in America's history who stood for truth, liberty, or freedom? Is it important that we learn about these kinds of people? Why or why not?

FEBRUARY 6—Why do you think adults or teenagers use drugs or drink alcohol to get drunk?

FEBRUARY 7—Do you think you need to feed your soul and your spirit every day just like you need to feed your physical body? Why or why not?

FEBRUARY 8—What is pride? Is it a good or bad thing? What is the opposite of pride?

FEBRUARY 9—What is one (or more) thing you would like to learn more about? Are there things that you find fascinating? If so, like what?

FEBRUARY 10—Is it possible for us to help other people around the world? Can you name some ways?

FEBRUARY 11—What is one *creative* way that each of us can be thoughtful to each other?

FEBRUARY 12—Who was Abraham Lincoln? Why do we celebrate his birthday? Is it important that we remember people like him? Why or why not?

FEBRUARY 13—Why do you think we wake up around the same time every day? Does it help us to listen to our body's internal clock? Why or why not?

FEBRUARY 14—Why do we celebrate Valentine's Day? Is it important to let other people know how we feel about them? Why or why not?

FEBRUARY 15—What makes someone a bully? (Nobody specific.) Is that good or bad? Why?

FEBRUARY 16—Can you name someone who single-handedly made a difference in the world? Do you believe that you could? Why or why not?

FEBRUARY 17—What is greed? Is it a good or a bad thing? What is the difference between greed and ambition?

FEBRUARY 18—Name a goal you have in life. Is it important to have goals? Why or why not?

FEBRUARY 19—Jesus asked his disciples, "Why do you look at the speck of saw dust in your brother's eye and pay no attention to the plank in your own eye?" (Matthew 7:3 NIV). What do you think he meant by this?

FEBRUARY 20—Is social media a good thing, a bad thing, or neutral? Why do you think that?

FEBRUARY 21—Who is someone you respect? How did he or she earn that respect?

FEBRUARY 22—Do you think America is a great country? Why or why not? Would you want to live in some other country instead?

FEBRUARY 23—What if two kids are fighting? What could you do? What if you were the President and two countries were fighting?

FEBRUARY 24—What makes someone a good member of a family? Is it the same as being on a team? If so, how?

FEBRUARY 25—Are we supposed to love *things* or just like them? What is the difference?

FEBRUARY 26—If you could change one thing about all people, what would it be?

FEBRUARY 27—Ellen Johnson Sirleaf is quoted as having said, "If your dreams don't scare you, they are not big enough." What do you think she meant by that? Do you agree with her? Why or why not?

FEBRUARY 28—Why do we have laws about when someone is old enough to be allowed to drive? Do you think it is good to have those laws? Why or why not?

FEBRUARY 29—What is a leap year? Why do you think we have them?

MARCH 1—What sport is your favorite to play? Which one is your favorite to watch? Why are they different, if they are?

MARCH 2—What is courage? Can you name a time when you were courageous? What about when you try something new? Does that take courage? If so, why?

MARCH 3—What if your teacher left the classroom during a test and the person sitting next to you asked for the answers? What would you do? What if the person were your best friend?

MARCH 4—What are some things that are sins? (Read Romans 1:29–32.) Did some of the things on this list surprise you? Can you see some of these things in yourself? Do you think that all sins are equal? Why or why not?

MARCH 5—What do you think it takes for someone to go from being good at something to being an expert at it? Why do you think that?

MARCH 6—Do you believe if someone is born into a poor family that he or she will (or even should) stay poor all of his or her life? Why or why not?

MARCH 7—What would you do if you had the opportunity to cheat on a test and you knew that no one would ever find out? Why?

MARCH 8—Do you think it is important to eat some healthy foods and get some exercise every day? Why or why not?

MARCH 9—Do you think that healthy foods are important for your brain as well as the rest of your body? How can you tell?

MARCH 10—Do you think that people are all the same or all different? Does being unique make us better or worse people? Why?

MARCH 11—Can you name two gifts or talents that God has given you? Can you see God's gifts in others? If so, like what?

MARCH 12—Name three fun hobbies that you like to do or would like to learn more about. Are hobbies important? Why or why not?

MARCH 13—Do you believe that we, as a family, know how to talk to each other and feel comfortable talking to each other? Why or why not?

MARCH 14—Can you remember a time when you thanked God for making you who you are? If so, what made you feel that way?

MARCH 15—When something bad happens, does that make God seem closer to you or farther away? Why?

MARCH 16—Have you ever met a celebrity or someone who has a lot of money? If so, how did it feel to meet him or her? Are famous and wealthy people really that much different than we are? If so, how?

MARCH 17—Who was St. Patrick? Do you think that it is silly that we have a day to celebrate him? Why or why not?

MARCH 18—Name, for each person here, one way that you don't respect him or her the way you should. What can you do to help change these feelings?

MARCH 19—Name at least one question that most people your age would love to be asked.

MARCH 20—Why do people fight? What does someone hope to accomplish in a fight?

MARCH 21—What do you think we need to do more of as a family? Why?

MARCH 22—What is the best things about spring? Why do you think God made the four seasons? Should there be more? Why or why not?

MARCH 23—Can you honestly admit that you are or were jealous of someone? If so, do you know why? How should we deal with jealousy?

MARCH 24—What is one thing that you are looking forward to right now? Why?

MARCH 25—Which do you like better, being alone or being with other people. Why?

MARCH 26—What is the most embarrassing thing that has ever happened to you? Do you think it's important to be able to laugh at yourself?

MARCH 27—What is a generation? Do they differ? If so, why? Are they the same in some ways too? How?

MARCH 28—What is Easter? Do you like Easter? Why or why not?

MARCH 29—Can you name a time when you were proud of yourself? If so, what made you proud? Why?

MARCH 30—Who is the funniest person you know? Why do you think he or she is so funny?

MARCH 31—Why do you think some people care so much about the brand of clothes they wear? Do you think that it is important? Why or why not?

Note to parents: Use the beginning of spring as a time to help your kids use the cues of nature to put off some old winter attitudes or habits and start with some "fresh" new beginnings.

APRIL 1—April Fools' Day is a day where we get to make practical jokes on other people. Is it okay to pull tricks on people sometimes? Why or why not? Are there times when it is appropriate and times when it is not? When do you think those times might be?

APRIL 2—Why do people in our society put so much importance on being thin? Do people in other countries feel this way too?

APRIL 3—Our society views the word "love" as a noun, an emotion. The authors of the Bible view the word "love" as a verb, something that you do. Do you believe there is significance in this difference? Why or why not?

APRIL 4—C. S. Lewis said, "Hardships often prepare ordinary people for an extraordinary destiny." Do you think that is true? Why or why not?

APRIL 5—Do you think there is value in failing something? Why or why not? If so, like what?

APRIL 6—Is there ever a time when a mistake that has been made should be left alone? Or is it never okay to knowingly leave an error in place? Why or why not?

APRIL 7—Memories have an emotion tied to them, which is why you remember them. Do you think it's a good thing or a bad thing that all memories have emotions tied to them? Why do you think that?

APRIL 8—Thomas Edison reportedly tried to make the light bulb 2,774 different times before he successfully made the light bulb. How many times would you try to make something before you gave up? What do you think made him keep trying?

APRIL 9—Do you think there is a reason that our bodies look different as we age? If so, why do you think that is?

APRIL 10—What makes someone a good friend? Are you one? How?

APRIL 11—Have you ever met someone who is afraid of something such as flying? How do you think he or she could overcome that fear?

APRIL 12—What is one thing you almost always seem to forget to do? Can you change that? If so, how could you? If not, why not?

APRIL 13—What is the best gift you've ever given to anyone? What made it so special?

APRIL 14—Abraham Lincoln once said, "I have been driven many times upon my knees by the overwhelming conviction that I had nowhere else to go." What do you think he meant by that?

APRIL 15—What would life be like if there was no television or other media devices? What would you do more of?

APRIL 16—Is your time valuable to you? Is it as valuable to you as money? Why or why not?

APRIL 17—Besides drugs and alcohol, are there other things that people get addicted to? Why do you think they get addicted to those things?

APRIL 18—If someone you know starts to argue with you, what are some ways you can defuse the argument? What if the person trying to argue with you is a stranger?

APRIL 19—Is it important to learn how to get along with other people? Why or why not?

APRIL 20—If I said, "Your hair is beautiful," is that a fact or my opinion? Is it important to be able to tell the difference between fact and opinion? Why or why not?

APRIL 21—One of our state's mottos says, "United we stand, divided we fall." Do you believe that is true? What about in our family?

APRIL 22—What is Earth Day? Is it important that everyone make an effort to keep the Earth healthy and beautiful? Why or why not?

APRIL 23—If someone gave you a million dollars, what would you do with the money?

APRIL 24—Where is the most beautiful place you have ever been? Why do you think it is so beautiful?

APRIL 25—What is the most incredible or awesome thing that you have ever seen? How did it make you feel?

APRIL 26—Can you name a time when you felt two very different emotions at the same time, such as love and hate or joy and sadness? Is it okay to feel that way? Why or why not?

APRIL 27—Do you feel that the sooner you grow up the better? Or, like Peter Pan, would you like to delay it as long as possible? Why?

APRIL 28—If you earned the exact same salary no matter what job you had, what would you do? Why?

APRIL 29—If you could eliminate any one flaw in your character, what would it be?

APRIL 30—If you found a bag marked with a bank's name with $10,000 inside, would you return it? If so, do you think that you would be better off because you were honest? Who else might benefit from your honesty? If not, why not?

MAY 1—If you could have one of the goals in your life met right now, would it make you happier? If so, how? What if all of them were met right now?

MAY 2—How do you know when you are feeling "stressed out"? What can you do to help calm yourself down when you realize what is happening?

MAY 3—Do you have any fears about your future? If so, what are your greatest fears about it? Are you excited about it too? Why or why not?

MAY 4—Have you ever heard someone say, "Oh, it's just a little white lie; it won't hurt anything"? Do you believe it is ever okay to lie? Why or why not?

MAY 5—What does the saying "waste not, want not" mean to you?

MAY 6—Are there people in your life who you trust? If so, what makes them trustworthy? If not, why not?

MAY 7—If you became a millionaire, how do you think it would change your life? What things would you want to stay the same?

MAY 8—The very first of the Ten Commandments is "You shall have no other gods before me" (Exodus 20:1–17). What other gods do you think the commandment is talking about?

MAY 9—Have you ever met someone who you thought was a horribly mean person only to find out later that he or she was going through a hard time in his or her life? Did this new information help you have a different opinion of the person? Why or why not?

MAY 10—Can you name three "healthy foods" for your soul?

MAY 11—Are daily routines important? Why or why not?

MAY 12—Have you ever had a friend you talked to every day? Were you closer to him or her than a friend who you spoke to only occasionally? Why do you think that is? What about Jesus? Would He be a closer friend if you spoke to Him every day?

MAY 13—Do you believe in ghosts or spirits? What about angels? Why or why not?

MAY 14—If you were to die tonight, what would you most regret not having said to someone?

MAY 15—How important are memories? Why? What purpose do you think they serve?

MAY 16—If a medicine were developed that would make obese people thin but would kill one out of every hundred people who took it, would you want it to be made available? Why or why not? What if the medicine cured a painful disease?

MAY 17—How important is money to you? How much would you have to be offered to leave the country and not come back?

MAY 18—Do you think that television and movies make us believe things that aren't true about the roles of men and women? Why or why not?

MAY 19—What is revenge? Are there situations when it is okay to act on feelings of revenge?

MAY 20—Bill Gates's mother said, "Each one of us has to start out with developing his or her own definition of success, and when we have these specific expectations of ourselves, we're more likely to live up to them." Do you think she is right? Why or why not?

MAY 21—If you could only have one or the other, would you rather have a poor but happy family or a successful career with no family? Why?

MAY 22— Is there anyone whom you admire? If so, what makes someone worth admiring?

MAY 23—A weakness is something about you that makes you less than perfect. Can you give an example of when God has used one of your weaknesses to benefit someone else?

MAY 24—If you truly loved someone, would you be willing to move to another country with him or her? What would make this easy or hard?

MAY 25—What is a character flaw? Do you think you have one? If so, what is it? Can you change this about yourself? If so, how?

MAY 26—If you could have one quality (such as intelligence, beauty, or exceptional patience) that you currently do not possess, what would it be? Why does this trait appeal to you?

MAY 27—If you married someone only to find out after a year that he or she was terminally ill, would you regret having married him or her? Why or why not?

MAY 28—What is envy? Do you envy anyone so much that you would be willing to change lives with him or her? If so, who? Would it surprise you to find out that person might like to trade with you? Why are other people's lives appealing to us?

MAY 29—How much do you value the lives of other creatures? Do you have a different response to the death of a butterfly than to the death of a spider? If so, why do you think that is?

MAY 30—Do you believe in the death sentence? Why or why not?

MAY 31—Do you have one special memory that you keep in your heart? Is it something you are willing to share with others? If not, why not?

JUNE 1—Ellen DeGeneres once said, "When you take risks, you learn that there will be times when you succeed and there will be times when you fail, and both are equally important." Do you agree or disagree with her? Why?

JUNE 2—Why do you think God allows some people to be extremely wealthy while others have nothing?

JUNE 3—Why do you think some people want to live here on earth forever? Would you want to? Which do you think is better—quality of life or quantity of life? Why?

JUNE 4—In the Bible, the apostle Paul says that God's plans for your life are even greater than what you can ever imagine? How does knowing that make you feel?

JUNE 5—What does it mean to be ostracized? Why do you think it is that many people fear being ostracized more than they fear death? Are there things you fear more than death?

JUNE 6—If you were asked by a friend to try a new food that sounded strange to you, what would you do?

JUNE 7—Do you believe it is important to have friends who are older than you are and friends who are younger than you are now? Why or why not?

JUNE 8—Do you have any big plans for your life? If so, do you know how you plan to achieve them?

JUNE 9—Is there anything or anyone in your life who you feel the most grateful for? Why or why not?

JUNE 10—One of your good friends or relatives tells you that he or she is dying of a fatal disease. How do you think that person would want you to handle the news?

JUNE 11—One of your best friends embarrasses you in public and makes fun of one of your best-kept secrets. How does this make you feel? And how would you handle the situation?

JUNE 12—Why do you think people exaggerate when telling a story? Do you think it adds to the story or detracts from it? Why?

JUNE 13—Do you accept advice from other people? If not, why not? If so, do you accept it from anyone or are you particular about whom you accept advice from? Why?

JUNE 14—Do you believe it is important to be punctual? Why or why not?

JUNE 15—Is yelling when you are angry helpful, harmful or both? Why? Why do you think people do it?

JUNE 16—Why do you think people have nightmares? Do they serve a purpose? What about good dreams?

JUNE 17—Are you the type of person who freely accepts help from others or are you the type who has a hard time accepting help from others even when you really need it? What makes you feel one way or the other?

JUNE 18—Is it easy or difficult for you to understand how other people can have a completely different point of view than your own? What do you think would help you to remain open-minded to see an issue from someone else's viewpoint?

JUNE 19—Does spending time alone help to refresh you? Why or why not?

JUNE 20—Often, when someone is given a fatal prognosis, he or she says that it is a blessing in disguise. Why do you think this person feels this way?

JUNE 21—How does it make you feel to see an animal neglected or abused? Why do you feel that way?

JUNE 22—Beverly Sills, a famous opera singer, once said, "There are no shortcuts to any place worth going." What do you think she meant by that? Do you feel the same way? Why or why not?

JUNE 23—Do you think that older people deserve to be respected simply because they are older? Why or why not?

JUNE 24—Do you feel that you are in control of your own destiny? Or do you feel that you are simply sailing along, without the ability to dictate your own path? What makes you feel this way?

JUNE 25—Do you believe that we need other people? Or do you think we are better off alone? Why?

JUNE 26—Do you think it is important for people to have dreams in life? Why or why not?

JUNE 27—Do you believe that it is important for you to live your life so that you receive honor from others here on earth? What about when you get to heaven?

JUNE 28—If someone asks you to do something that you have never tried before, are you excited at the idea? Or does it make you anxious? Why?

JUNE 29—Why do you think some people feel it necessary to criticize others? Do you think that it is wrong to be critical? Why or why not? What if they are being critical of you?

JUNE 30—What are emotions? Why do you think we have them?

Note to parents: Take some of those summer evenings when you don't have to worry about getting up early for school to lie outside and look up at the stars. Ask some questions out there too. Kids will talk more openly and tell you some of their deepest thoughts in the dark.

JULY 1—Do you believe the saying, "Beauty is only skin deep"? What do you think people mean when they say that?

JULY 2—Do you believe that we can make our lives better (either individually or collectively) by studying other people's mistakes and successes in history? Why or why not?

JULY 3—Why do you think so many teenagers consider committing suicide? Do you think all teens have something in common that makes them more susceptible to thoughts of suicide? If so, what do you think it is?

JULY 4—What is Independence Day? Why do we celebrate it? Does it seem strange for you to think that people from other countries do not understand why we have this holiday or don't even know what it is?

JULY 5—When the men who wrote the Declaration of Independence declared the United States free from England, do you think they only declared us free "from" being under Britain's rule or do you think they declared us independent "for" something else also? If so, what do you think they might have hoped for the people of this country?

JULY 6—Do you believe that your brain and your emotions can lie to you? Why or why not?

JULY 7—Do you feel that it is better to have a lot of casual friends or just one or two really good friends? Why do you feel that way?

JULY 8—What do you think people mean when they say, "If it doesn't kill you, it will make you stronger"? Do you believe this is true? Why or why not?

JULY 9—Do you believe that it is hard to be in your teenage years? Why or why not?

JULY 10—Do you believe that it is all right to date and/or marry someone of another race? Why or why not? What about another religion?

JULY 11—Do you believe that you should date someone even if you know that you would never marry him or her? Why or why not?

JULY 12—Do you feel differently when you see a man cry versus when you see a woman cry? Why or why not?

JULY 13—Do you think people should or should not get tattoos? Why do you feel that way?

JULY 14—What do you think it means to "lay down your life for your friends"?

JULY 15—Do you expect people to act differently than you act yourself? Why or why not? What if they are older or younger than you are?

JULY 16—Do you believe someone should have the right to kill him or herself? What if they were dying from a terrible disease? What if they asked someone to assist them?

JULY 17—Do you believe the saying, "It always pays to be honest"? Why or why not?

JULY 18—Do you believe that it is important to be well organized? Why or why not? Is there such a thing as being too organized? If so, when? If not, why not?

JULY 19—Do you believe smarter people live happier lives? Why or why not?

JULY 20—Is there anything that you simply hate doing but have to do anyway? If so, is there anything you could do to make the experience more enjoyable?

JULY 21—Do you think people can become obsessed with looking at themselves in the mirror? If so, why do you think this happens?

JULY 22—What do you think people say to themselves right before they steal something?

JULY 23—How old do you believe someone needs to be before having his or her first sexual partner? Are there other factors that need to be taken into consideration as well? If so, what?

JULY 24—If you went to a movie with a friend and during the film you started to become offended or uncomfortable with the movie's content, would you be willing to walk out? Why or why not? What if your friend wanted to leave?

JULY 25—What constitutes an intimate relationship? For example, can you be intimate simply by kissing, or does it have to go farther than that?

JULY 26—Do you believe that you can put a monetary value on friendship? Why or why not?

JULY 27—What do you think are some of the best things about life?

JULY 28—How important is it for you to receive compliments? Why? How important is it for you to give compliments? Why?

JULY 29—Do you believe there is any value in going over—or rehearsing—in your mind what you will say during a difficult conversation? Why or why not?

JULY 30—Some people define stupidity as "doing the same thing over and over expecting different results." What do you think this means? Do you agree? Why or why not?

JULY 31—Why do some people have routines, like always sleeping on the same side of the bed? Do you think these routines serve a purpose? Why or why not? What is the difference between a routine and a discipline?

AUGUST 1—Is the first day of a new school year a good thing or a bad thing or both? Why?

AUGUST 2—Do you believe you were placed in this particular time period for a reason? If so, why? Would you rather have lived in some other period in history? Why or why not?

AUGUST 3—How important is it to you to be dressed appropriately? If you were to go to a party either very overdressed or very underdressed, would it affect your ability to enjoy the party? Why or why not?

AUGUST 4—In our society, physical touching among casual acquaintances is somewhat taboo. Yet, in many societies, it is perfectly acceptable. How do you feel about it?

AUGUST 5—Has someone you have known ever done something that you thought was totally out of character for that person (for example, cheated on a test or stolen something)? If so, how did it make you feel and how did you handle those feelings?

AUGUST 6—Do you believe it is important for you to be a good listener for your friends? Why or why not?

AUGUST 7—It is said that most people overestimate what they can accomplish in one year but underestimate what they can accomplish in ten years. What do you think you could accomplish in the next ten years if you started planning for it now?

AUGUST 8—When you have an extremely important decision to make, are you more likely to pray about it, logically weigh the pros against the cons, follow your intuition, or just flip a coin? Why?

AUGUST 9—How important is it for your friends to be honest with you? What if they were honest with you and you didn't like the answer?

AUGUST 10—The first four of the Ten Commandments deal with our relationship with God. The next six deal with our relationships with each other. Do you believe it is significant that all ten deal with relationships? If so, in what way?

AUGUST 11—Most adults say that their family is much more important to them than their careers. Do you plan to balance a career and your family life? If so, how?

AUGUST 12—Do you believe that a person's friends are a reflection on who he or she is? Why or why not?

AUGUST 13—Is there ever a time when it is appropriate not to forgive someone who has wronged you? Why or why not? If you do forgive someone, does that mean you also have to trust him or her? Why or why not?

AUGUST 14—Have you ever experienced an epiphany or a paradigm shift? If so, do you feel that it made you a better person? Why or why not?

AUGUST 15—Do you believe that advertisers have a powerful influence (either positive or negative) on society? Why or why not?

AUGUST 16—Do you believe that unpleasant childhood experiences help to shape our personalities for the better? Why or why not?

AUGUST 17—Have you ever done favors for someone because you thought he or she would like you more if you did? If so, did doing the favors accomplish the intended result? Whether it did or didn't, how did you feel afterward?

AUGUST 18—Do you believe that you will try to raise your children differently than the way you were raised? Why or why not?

AUGUST 19—Have you ever sacrificed your own desires for someone else's, only to have that person seem ungrateful? How did this make you feel? Are you gracious when someone makes sacrifices for you?

AUGUST 20—Do you believe that it is good for your soul to occasionally have days when you have no plans and can stay in your pajamas all day if you wanted? Why or why not?

AUGUST 21—Do you believe that there are situations when a woman should have the right to get an abortion? Why or why not?

AUGUST 22—If a person is terminally ill, should someone (such as a doctor or a family member) have the right to keep the knowledge of the illness a secret from that person? Why or why not? What if the person was already a hypochondriac and either the doctor or the family felt it was in the interest of the person's health to keep this knowledge a secret?

AUGUST 23—How important is it for you to live your life so that, as you grow older, you can look back on your life without regrets? Why?

AUGUST 24—How much of our self-identity do you think is linked to what we see in the mirror? Would you feel like a completely different person if your physical appearance was suddenly and dramatically changed either for the worse or for the better?

AUGUST 25—If you were really in love with someone and planning to marry him or her but all of your family and friends thought you were making a big mistake, would you go through with it? Why or why not?

AUGUST 26—If you could go on your dream vacation, where would you go? Would you want to take someone with you? If so, who?

AUGUST 27—Eleanor Roosevelt once said, "No one can make you feel inferior without your consent." What do you think she meant by that?

AUGUST 28—In a baseball game, every player knows how he or she can win and what he or she each needs to do to win the game. Is that true in a family as well? What do you think it means for us as a family to get a win?

AUGUST 29—Do you think that men and women are the same or different? In what ways? Why do you think God made them this way?

AUGUST 30—Many professional athletes use a training tool called "visualization" to practice performing their sport at their best. Do you believe it really works? If so, do you think other people can use that tool in other areas of life with much success as well? Why or why not?

AUGUST 31—King David said in the Psalms that Creation declares God's glory in every language. What do you think that means? Do you believe that is true? Why or why not?

SEPTEMBER 1—Can you think of someone who, in a short amount of time, had a big impact on your life? What was it about this person that made him or her make such an impression on you?

SEPTEMBER 2— Will Rogers once said, "You never get a second chance to make a first impression." Do you believe that this is true? Why or why not?

SEPTEMBER 3—Have you ever been in a situation when you have gone out of your way to do something nice for someone and that person failed to thank you for your effort? How did it make you feel? Will your feeling affect you doing something nice for that person again?

SEPTEMBER 4—Is there ever a good reason to kill someone? Why do you think that?

SEPTEMBER 5—How can you be the best version of you there is?

SEPTEMBER 6—What is the best present you or someone you know was given? What made it so great?

SEPTEMBER 7—What are the benefits of search engines such as Google? Are there detriments too? If so, like what?

SEPTEMBER 8—Do you like to talk on the phone? Why or why not?

SEPTEMBER 9—Which do you like better, summer or winter? Why?

SEPTEMBER 10—Besides exchanging gifts, what is one thing that we do as a family during the holidays that you look forward to every year?

SEPTEMBER 11—Do you think it is important for us to always remember what happened on 9/11? Why or why not?

SEPTEMBER 12—What if you have a teacher or a coworker you don't like? What can you do about that? What can't you do?

SEPTEMBER 13—Is it easy or hard to get out of bed on Christmas Day? How could you get up with that kind of excitement and anticipation every day?

SEPTEMBER 14—Is someone the same person at forty years old that he or she was at twenty-five or fifteen? Why do you think that is?

SEPTEMBER 15—What is unconditional love? Do you know anyone who can love you that way?

SEPTEMBER 16—If someone gives you a compliment, do you believe him or her? Why or why not?

SEPTEMBER 17—Do you think you can tell a lot about a person by what he or she thinks is funny? Why or why not?

SEPTEMBER 18—In some cultures, it is seen as scandalous to expose your shoulders in public. In the 1800s in America, women were forbidden to expose their ankles in public. Where do you think those cultural rules come from? Do you agree with them? Why or why not?

SEPTEMBER 19—When someone is born into a family that has millions of dollars, what do you think that person should do with his or her life?

SEPTEMBER 20—Why do you think God allows evil in the world?

SEPTEMBER 21—What is your favorite thing to do? Do you like to do it alone, with people, or both?

SEPTEMBER 22—Do you think it is important to keep an open mind in life? Why or why not?

SEPTEMBER 23—If you could ask someone in heaven one question, what would it be?

SEPTEMBER 24—What is one thing you think people in America take for granted and why do you think that?

SEPTEMBER 25—If someone said to you, "Go hard or go home," what do you think that means? Do you agree with that philosophy? Why or why not?

SEPTEMBER 26—Do you believe it is important to try things you've never tried before? Why or why not?

SEPTEMBER 27—Do you think you should give people the benefit of the doubt? If so, why? If not, why not?

SEPTEMBER 28—What do you think is the difference between grace and mercy?

SEPTEMBER 29—Do you think it is important that our President believes in God? Why or why not?

SEPTEMBER 30—Name two ways you can show respect. (After everyone answers) does it make you feel better or worse to show respect to someone else?

Note to parents: As the new school year gets under way and new friendships are formed, remember to help each child mourn the loss of some old friendships that he or she may have had to say goodbye to last year (including favorite teachers). Adults have an easier time than children do realizing that friendships might only be seasonal. Take a few moments occasionally and ask each of your kids, "How's your heart? Is it okay?"

OCTOBER 1—Do you think it is important that we recognize our own weaknesses? Why do you think that?

OCTOBER 2—Do you think all people are equal no matter where they come from or the color of their skin or their gender? Why do you feel that way?

OCTOBER 3—Do you believe it is important to always have something to look forward to? Why do you think that?

OCTOBER 4—Is it ever okay to judge someone? If so, when do you think that?

OCTOBER 5—Do you think it is important that we do something fun every day? Why or why not?

OCTOBER 6—What would you say to a friend who told you that his or her mom and dad were getting a divorce?

OCTOBER 7—Do you think it is a good idea to keep a journal? If so, why do you think that?

OCTOBER 8—King David said to God, "Your word is a lamp to my feet and a light to my path" (Psalm 119:105). Do you believe that too? Why or why not?

OCTOBER 9—If we all want what is best for our country, why do you think people have such different ideas about how to make that happen?

OCTOBER 10—Do you think it's important that we study history? Why or why not?

OCTOBER 11—What is your favorite subject in school? What do you like about it?

OCTOBER 12—Is money a good thing or a bad thing or both? Why do you think that?

OCTOBER 13—Some people believe in reincarnation. Do you? Why or why not?

OCTOBER 14—What are taxes? Are they a good thing or a bad thing? Why do you think that?

OCTOBER 15—If you could give everyone in the world one thing, what would it be?

OCTOBER 16—Do you think Americans should be able to speak more languages? Why or why not?

OCTOBER 17—If you could travel in time, where would you go and why?

OCTOBER 18—What is the best story you have ever heard? What made it so great?

OCTOBER 19—Why do you think we have imaginations? Do some people have more imagination than others? Why do you think that is?

OCTOBER 20—What is self-confidence? Is there a good time to have it and a good time not to have it? Why do you think that?

OCTOBER 21—What is etiquette? Is it important to have it? Why do you think that?

OCTOBER 22—What makes you really mad? What can you do with that anger?

OCTOBER 23—Do you know people who have really big families, such as five or six brothers and sisters? Do you think they are happier because they have a big family? Why or why not?

OCTOBER 24—If you could know one thing about your future, what would it be? Do you think it is good that we don't know much about our futures? Why or why not?

OCTOBER 25—Sometimes people will say that something bad that happened to them is the best thing that ever happened? Why do you think they say that?

OCTOBER 26—Is there a difference between a dream and a goal? If so, do you know how to turn a dream into a goal? If so, how?

OCTOBER 27—Why do you think some people who are born into terrible circumstances still become really successful in life but others who are born into families with everything are never able to find success or happiness?

OCTOBER 28—Why do you think there are so many different kinds of plants and animals?

OCTOBER 29—If you could ask God one question, what would it be?

OCTOBER 30—Is there something you are looking forward to? Why?

OCTOBER 31—The word "Halloween" came from when people used to say, "Happy Hallowed Eve," because tomorrow, November 1, is traditionally the most holy day of the year, when the people in many Christian denominations celebrate All Saints' Day. Why do you think our culture has lost that meaning for this word over time? Do other words lose their original meaning? Can you name one?

NOVEMBER 1—Do you think it's okay to play tricks on people? Why or why not?

NOVEMBER 2—What is a vote? Do you think people should vote? Why or why not?

NOVEMBER 3—What is shame? Why do we feel ashamed of something we might have done? Do you think we are supposed to learn something from that feeling? If so, what?

NOVEMBER 4—Where do you think joy comes from? Is it different than happiness? Why or why not?

NOVEMBER 5—Why are some people more patient than others? Is it good to be patient or not really? Why do you think that?

NOVEMBER 6—Where is the most peaceful place you know? What makes it so peaceful?

NOVEMBER 7—Who is the kindest person you know? What makes him or her so kind?

NOVEMBER 8—Name three things that you think are good. What makes them good?

NOVEMBER 10—What does it mean to be humble? Are there times when it is good to be humble and times when it is not good to be humble? When?

NOVEMBER 11—Today is Veteran's Day. Do you think it's important that we honor our veterans? Why or why not?

NOVEMBER 12—What is self-discipline? Is it a good thing or a bad thing to have self-discipline? Why?

NOVEMBER 13—Can music change the way you feel? Why do you think that is?

NOVEMBER 14—Where does wind come from? Do you think it makes things any less cool because scientists can explain where it comes from? Why or why not?

NOVEMBER 15—Are guns good things or bad things or both? Why do you think that?

NOVEMBER 16—Do you know people who are generous? What makes them generous? Can people be too generous? Why or why not?

NOVEMBER 17—Do you like it when other people remember your birthday? Why or why not?

NOVEMBER 18—Do you think it is important to be flexible in life? Why or why not?

NOVEMBER 19—There is a saying that says, "If you don't stand for something, you will fall for anything." What do you think that means? Do you agree with that statement?

NOVEMBER 20—What do you think all good stories have in common?

NOVEMBER 21—Are little chores, such as making your bed, important or a waste of time? Why do you think that?

NOVEMBER 22—Thanksgiving Day is a United States holiday where we remember the Pilgrims gave thanks to God for their first harvest in 1641. Do you think this is an important holiday? Why or why not?

NOVEMBER 23—You've probably heard it said that laughter is the best medicine. Do you think that is true? Why or why not?

NOVEMBER 24—What is hope? Is it important to always have some? Why or why not?

NOVEMBER 25—Why do you think there are several different religions in the world?

NOVEMBER 26—Why can't we choose who our relatives are? Do you think it's important to stay close to them because they are relatives? Why or why not?

NOVEMBER 27—What if a person you want to be friends with doesn't want to be your friend? What can you do? Are there things you shouldn't do?

NOVEMBER 28—Why do you think there is music?

NOVEMBER 29—What is your definition of success? (after everyone answers) Is it okay if our answers are different?

NOVEMBER 30—Has there ever been a time when you had to wait for a really long time for something? Did the wait make the result better? Why or why not?

DECEMBER 1—Are there questions we won't ever know the answers to? If so, like what?

DECEMBER 2—Name something you had to work really hard to get. (After everyone answers) did having to work hard for it make receiving it better? Why or why not?

DECEMBER 3—Do you think people should get married when they are young or when they are older? Why do you think that?

DECEMBER 4—Name something you learned today. Do you think it is a good idea to learn something new every day? Why or why not?

DECEMBER 5—What is the scariest thing you've ever done?

DECEMBER 6—What do you like about traveling? What don't you like about traveling?

DECEMBER 7—President Franklin Roosevelt called December 7 "a date which will live in infamy." Do you know why he said that? Is that important for us to remember?

DECEMBER 8—Do you think it's important to visit other countries? Why or why not?

DECEMBER 9—If someone asks you, "What do you want to be when you grow up?" what do you say? Is it okay if you say that you don't know? Why or why not?

DECEMBER 10—Who is someone you would like to meet and why?

DECEMBER 11—Do you like things to be planned out in detail or do you like things to be spontaneous?

DECEMBER 12—What is something strange that you would like to do some day?

DECEMBER 13—Why do you think people believe in superstitions? Do you have any?

DECEMBER 14—Are there things that you are scared of? Do you think it is good to be scared of some things? Why or why not?

DECEMBER 15—What are morals? Do you think all people have the same morals or different? Why do you think that?

DECEMBER 16—Do you think it is important to share? Is it sometimes okay not to share? If so, when?

DECEMBER 17—What do you like least about yourself? What can you do to change that?

DECEMBER 18—What is the first thing you notice about other people?

DECEMBER 19—If you could try out any job for one day, what would you like to try?

DECEMBER 20—What is the stupidest thing you've ever done? Did you know it was stupid when you did it?

DECEMBER 21—Do you think it is important to forgive yourself when you mess up? Why do you think that?

DECEMBER 22—Do you think all people are equally valuable, or do you think some people are more valuable than others? Why do you think that?

DECEMBER 23—Do you think people can control their own destiny?

DECEMBER 24—If you could learn one new thing this coming year, what would you like to learn?

DECEMBER 25—What would you say to someone who told you that he or she didn't celebrate Christmas?

DECEMBER 26—Do you think people who are born in very poor countries should move to another place? Or should they try to stay and make that country better?

DECEMBER 27—What is one of your favorite questions to ask new friends or to get a conversation going?

DECEMBER 28—If someone were to make a movie about your life, who do you hope would play you?

DECEMBER 29—What do you think is something that is very unattractive in a person?

DECEMBER 30—Do you think it's good that we start a new year every 365 days? What is good or bad about it?

DECEMBER 31—Do you think you can learn something about yourself if you take some time and evaluate this past year? If so, like what?

Note to parents: As this year ends, help your kids look to the hope and promises of what the new year will bring.

Addendum: Questions for Preschoolers

For families with preschoolers, here are a few questions you can include that will help your little ones feel included in the discussions.

- What is your favorite color? Has it always been your favorite? Is it okay to change your mind or to have more than one favorite? Why do you think so?
- When was the last time you were so excited that you felt like shouting out loud? Why were you so excited?
- If you could keep only one of your toys or things, which one would you keep? Why?
- What is your favorite movie? What makes it your favorite?
- What can you do when you are sad or depressed to help yourself feel better?
- Who do you think loves you? Name as many people you can think of who love you!
- Everyone has to make his or her silliest face or do a silly dance. Is it good or bad to be silly sometimes? Why? Are

there times when it's okay to be silly and times when it's not?

- Who is your favorite movie character? Why do you like that character so much?
- What is the best thing that ever happened to you? What made it so wonderful?
- Who is your most favorite person in the whole world? Why do you like him or her so much?

Remember, the way to get better answers is to ask better questions. Please join our community of parents at www.food4thought.family and let us help you, encourage you, and pray for you.